V

Catholic

Twenty-One People Give Their Own Reasons

George R. Szews

ACTA Publications
Chicago, Illinois

Why I Am Catholic
Twenty-One People Give Their Own Reasons
by George R. Szews

Edited by Jean K. Larkin
Cover Design by Tom A. Wright
Typesetting by Garrison Publications

Special thanks to the men and women who contributed their own reasons.

Published by ACTA Publications,
Assisting Christians To Act,
4848 N. Clark Street, Chicago, IL 60640,
312-271-1030.

Library of Congress Catalog number: 95-083431

ISBN: 0-87946-136-5

Printed in the United States of America

00 99 98 97 96 5 4 3 2 1 First Edition

Table of Contents

Introduction

If I had to give my reason for being Catholic, it would be that I can't remember ever not being Catholic. I don't mean that to be as glib as it sounds. There was a time when I didn't go to church; yet I knew I was still Catholic. There are times when I'm angry with God; yet I am still Catholic. There are times when I grow frustrated with the Catholic Church; yet I remain Catholic. There are times when I feel others drawing lines in the sand and pushing me out of *their* Catholic Church; yet I hold my ground. It is *my* Church too; it is somehow me.

One thing I'm sure of is that the Catholic Church was a gift to me. I didn't pick it while cruising a spiritual mall, and I didn't hint to my parents as my birthday approached that what I *really wanted* was a good Church to grow old in. My parents, my relatives, the people in the town where I grew up all gave me the Catholic Church as part of my identity, because they believed and thought it would be good for me to believe also. From my birth, the subtleties of what it means to be Catholic were poured into my soul.

I admit my experience of being a "cradle" Catholic contradicts one of the highest values of the culture I live in: choice. That doesn't bother me much. I've learned there is more to my life than the choices I make (thank God). Some of the choices I've made haven't been all that hot, and there is little solace in saying, "At least *I* made them."

This is not to say I don't feel responsible or don't feel free. The more my Catholicity sinks into me, the more accountable for my freedom I become. There is something in me that always tingles when I hear, "To the one to whom much has been given, much will be expected." Because I'm Catholic, I've learned to balance that noble calling against the certainty of God's grace.

Being Catholic means you're never alone and you're never on your own. There are literally millions of sisters and brothers throughout history and around the world bonded to one another by the fact of being Catholic.

Here are twenty-one people I know, who give their own reasons for being Catholic.

(Rev.) George R. Szews
Eau Claire, Wisconsin

Phyllis

is a wife, mother, grandmother, and volunteer.

My Catholic identity was formed in the thirties, forties, and fifties—when the external trappings of religion clearly distinguished "us" from "them." The Catholic religious tradition wrapped snugly around us: novenas to Our Mother of Perpetual Help, May altars, First Friday Masses, regular days of fast and abstinence, Gregorian chant, indulgences, Forty Hours Devotion, dimly-lit churches for confession on Saturday afternoons.

Being Catholic was, of course, more than those outward signs. There were Catholic dogmas and theology, Catholic virtue and action. All in all, we tended to know who we were—religiously speaking. We knew what we believed in and hoped for.

Now many of the external forms have been peeled away, and we are asked to concentrate on the essentials of Catholic life. That takes more effort, but I find assurance in two special lines from Isaiah—Chapter 42 (or thereabouts). They are phrases I am familiar with because they are in the cycle of Sunday readings, and I am a lector—a role I could only have played in the new Church!

"I have grasped you by the hand . . . I have called you by name." I have the distinct feeling God has me by the hand, often having to pull me along, saying all the while, "C'mon, Phyllis, c'mon now."

FOR REFLECTION OR DISCUSSION

1. What rituals or family traditions meant the most to you in your childhood?
2. Why were they important to you?
3. What (if anything) has replaced them?

Dolly

is a wife, mother, grandmother, and business owner who says she understands how people can leave the Catholic Church for a while . . . and why they come back.

I was planted in the Catholic Church. I attended Catholic elementary school, then went on to four years in a Catholic girls' academy. All of my early childhood revolved around my parish, St. Vincent de Paul. My parents were not just "Sunday Mass Catholics." We attended *all* the services and events in our parish.

I grew up in a Catholic Church that was strict—everything was either black or white. There were no questions, just acceptance. Then came Vatican II and so many changes and, I think, a real invitation to me to fuller participation in the Church.

All of my Catholic life has not been easy. As recently as five years ago my integrity was questioned by some in my parish. How could those with whom I prayed, with whom I shared joys and tears for so many years, hurt me so deeply? I felt disowned by the very people who made up part of my identity, by people I considered part of my family. I didn't want to go to church anymore. For a while, I went to other Catholic churches in the area; sometimes I didn't go to church at all. Yet even as I continued to pray alone, there was a growing emptiness in me. I needed to be part of a real community. I couldn't be "Catholic" without "being with others."

It took time, but I believe the Lord led me to the Catholic Church and gave me my "family" again. This journey has made me feel even more responsible to share my faith with others, to be a role model for my children, my grandchildren and other women. I feel challenged to continue to grow, to learn, and to pass on this great faith that has been given to me.

FOR REFLECTION OR DISCUSSION

1. Have you ever felt rejected or alienated from a group of people you love?
2. How has God been present—or absent—to you during that time?
3. What does the word *community* mean to you? Where do you find your community?

Patrick

is a physician and the proud father of five children. He hopes his mother never sees this essay.

It was thirteen years ago when I decided I really wanted to be a Catholic. I was twenty-six years old. Eight months previously I had become a father for the first time. My son was a big, happy bruiser of a child. Because I was still in medical training, we had little money and I had even less free time. We lived in a small apartment with beat-up or borrowed furniture, and we drove a junker. But they were great times.

My wife and I had gotten off to a great start in our marriage, and our son was the greatest source of joy in our lives. He was gorgeous, adorable, and handsome. He looked just like me! He had unusual motor skills, walked at six months, and was athletically gifted—just like me. Most importantly, he was clearly a genius—again like me!

I had been raised in a large, conservative, Irish-Catholic family. By this point in my life I had attended nineteen years of Catholic school. Somewhere along the way, though, the Church and I had gone separate ways. I hadn't attended Mass more than once or twice since my marriage to my nominally Presbyterian wife.

As my wife and I watched this wonderful child grow so rapidly, however, we desperately wanted him to have the opportunity to realize the potential of all his gifts. How were we going to provide him with the moral framework he would need? Where would he learn the lessons and values that would be necessary for him to become a happy, whole adult? How and what would he learn about God?

I came to understand that, regardless of my problems with the Church, I had to make sure this child received the same gifts my parents had given me. Maybe he would do more with his faith than I had done with mine.

Late in the summer of my son's first year, I persuaded a reluctant priest in a parish I had never attended to baptize the largest seven-month-old boy ever brought to the baptismal font. I'm glad that priest gave us a chance. Joe's baptism was as much mine as his.

FOR REFLECTION OR DISCUSSION

1. In your own life, what or who do you think had the most significant impact in forming your values?
2. If you could teach just one important value to a child, what would it be?
3. What institution or community of people will help you transmit your values to the next generation?

Donna

is an author of children's books and a relatively new Catholic.

I became Catholic because my mother-in-law insisted on evangelizing everyone with her Catholicism—to the point of turning people off.

I grew up Protestant and found comfort and strength in my denomination. When I married, I certainly did not need to learn new ways to worship and believe. I had my own.

It was okay with me if my mother-in-law wanted to pray in bed for two hours every morning or observe obscure "holy" days. It was okay if she prayed the Rosary for hours in the car when we went on a trip together. As far as I was concerned, she could have her Church and odd religious practices. I had what I needed and wanted.

God works in strange ways, however, always ahead of us. God knew the journey I had to take for the next six years. I believe now God knew that if I was to be the kind of person, mother, and friend I wanted to be, I needed to move toward Catholicism.

Slowly the walls tumbled. I opened myself to new ways of thinking and seeing the world, and my faith not only changed but became very real to me. Many tell me they sense my new-found spirituality, for which I can claim no credit. Now I'm proud to say I lie in bed every morning and pray and, although I don't pray the Rosary while I travel like my mother-in-law, I do pray when I'm in my car. God does work in strange ways.

FOR REFLECTION OR DISCUSSION

1. How have other people influenced your growth and development?
2. Are you open to new ways of thinking and seeing the world?
3. What is your own prayer routine?

Larry

has been employed for 28 years with a city police department.

I grew up Methodist. My father and grandfather were ordained ministers in the Methodist Church. I came to Catholicism slowly, and then only after an ill-conceived notion of rejection.

When I was preparing for marriage to a woman who was Catholic, the Air Force chaplain told me that if I didn't sign the written promise to raise our children Catholic the wedding would not take place. I was stunned. I had heard of such things but didn't believe they could be true. I didn't understand and felt outraged.

For some time, my prospective parents-in-law were against the impending marriage. They were not alone; my parents felt the same way. My future wife and I, however, believed a mixed marriage could work if the two of us would just keep our focus on love and understanding. But the sense of rejection kept growing inside of me.

Happily, my feelings did not go unchecked. My father was invited by the parish priest who married us to share in the wedding liturgy and pronounced us husband and wife. Later, when we were members of our neighborhood Catholic Church, both of us were invited to serve on the religious education board. Finally I felt God inviting me to ask about formally joining the Catholic Church. I thought all I'd have to do would be to walk into the rectory and sign on the dotted line.

On that day, which I still remember so clearly, I went into the pastor's office, told my story, and took out my pen. The priest, however, held up his hand and told me to wait. He gave me a book to read and invited me to come back in the fall. I felt like I had been rejected—again.

As it turned out, I was wrong. I participated in the RCIA process for people who wanted to become Catholics, which gave me spiritual food I had not tasted before. My in-laws were wonderful and accepting. My parents in turn accepted my wife and her Catholicism. Our two sons joined us in church.

"Invited" is the best way for me to describe my sense of Catholicism. I never felt pressured or obligated by the Church to join. I did feel invited in a special way. That sense of invitation is why I relish the RCIA process, which is offered every year in most parishes.

What I had perceived as rejection was really God's way of telling me to wait and understand the Church's invitation and acceptance of who I am, not what I was.

FOR REFLECTION OR DISCUSSION

1. Think of a time when you wanted to be invited to join a group or an organization. How did you feel if no one asked you?
2. How did you feel if you were asked?
3. Do you invite others to join you in things in which you are interested and involved?

Janeway

is a business woman, drives a convertible, and is determined.

Oklahoma had no Republican ticket. The Catholic population was only three percent of the state's total. My family was Republican and Catholic. We were strict, devout Catholics who said the Rosary and went to daily Mass . . . and we wrote in the names of Republicans on ballots.

We felt the sting of prejudice more than once. Our small parish clung together against the "rages of Protestantism." Ecumenism was still another twenty years away. The only time I set foot in a Protestant church was when a neighbor girl invited me to hear a gospel group performing there. I can't remember my family having any close friends who were not Catholic.

The Church I knew was rigid and determined. Divorce didn't happen except in extreme cases, and then remarriage was never a possibility. My mother led a life of deprivation and loneliness because of this, but I have forgiven the Church.

When I went away to Marquette University, the Jesuits opened up all kinds of incredible possibilities to me. The Church to which I was introduced was kind, open, loving, playful, and forgiving. One of my friends, a Jesuit, told me, "Play is the highest form of prayer." I was stunned and have forever looked at the Church in a different light.

After my marriage of twenty-one years ended in divorce and I was contemplating marriage to a Protestant, my pastor urged me to seek an annulment: "How would you feel not being able to receive the sacraments?" he asked.

"I can't imagine being invited to dinner and not allowed to eat!" I replied. He smiled and said: "You're right. I know how much the Church means to you, and I want you to know the Church will not turn its back on you!" What a wonderful, loving attitude.

The reason I am Catholic is that the Church I know today is loving, forgiving, accepting, welcoming—no matter what! I am grateful for such a spiritual home.

FOR REFLECTION OR DISCUSSION

1. When you are challenged on your values or beliefs, how do you react?
2. Think of a time when you formed an opinion about a situation before you knew all the facts. How right were you?
3. What is forgiveness, and how have you experienced it in your life?

Barbara

has held several jobs since the one described here. Presently she is a librarian and freelance writer.

Though Catholicism was chosen for me at infancy by my parents, *staying* Catholic has been largely the work of grace, grace appearing in human form. Whenever I have drifted from the Church, I have been drawn back by people who reminded me what being Catholic is all about.

In childhood I was an obedient Catholic, but I grew into an idealistic, self-righteous adolescent, full of criticism of the Church. At age sixteen I met someone who showed me that my idealism was really a passion for justice, which fit in beautifully with being Catholic.

That summer my best friend and I got our first "real" jobs, for minimum wage—$1.60 an hour! Together we were to go door to door circulating fund-raising envelopes for the Cystic Fibrosis Association.

Each morning we had to pick up envelopes at a home in a poor, unfamiliar neighborhood. During our weeks on that job we chatted with the young man who lived in the house, a cheerful fellow who was often mowing the lawn when we stopped by. He kidded around with us but also asked our opinions about the Vietnam War, nuclear weapons, and social problems in America. When we asked this mysterious man who he was and what he did, he just laughed and said that he mowed the lawn.

Once he told us the story of St. Francis, how as a young man Francis rejected his family's wealth by taking off his clothes in the town square and striding off naked into the woods, where he lived ever after, devoting his life to the poor. I was impressed. I later learned this man "who just mowed the lawn" was a Catholic priest who spent his time feeding the poor and working for peace. He was, and still is, part of a social action community that takes in the homeless and runs a soup kitchen. When I met him at such an impressionable age, he was a stirring example to me of the Church in action.

People like him, as well as others more famous, such as Thomas Merton, Oscar Romero, and Mother Theresa, remind me what a strong and positive influence the Catholic Church can have on its members and the world. But it is not only the heroes and extraordinary people who keep me in the Church. All around me are Catholics who keep my faith alive on an ongoing basis. I see them every weekend.

FOR REFLECTION OF DISCUSSION

1. Have you ever revolted against or rejected anyone or anything? What, if anything, brought you back?
2. Who are the people you most admire? Why?
3. What do you do to promote peace and justice within your family, parish, neighborhood, world?

Peter

is a mail carrier who reads a lot.

Like most Roman Catholics, I am Catholic because I was born into a Catholic family, church, and culture. Rationally, this may not be a good reason to be Catholic; however, the Vietnamese Buddhist monk, Thich Nhat Hahn, said in a speech at the 1993 Parliament of the World Religions that "our spiritual journey will move more smoothly forward if we return to our religious roots."

One good reason I am Catholic is that the roots of my Church reach out so far and wide. Contrary to the worries of some of my fellow Catholics, you still can be a "cafeteria Catholic" and be a good Catholic. I'm not talking about morals, dogmas, or canon law but of ways to find, listen, and talk to God. Each of our spiritual temperaments is different and each results in a different path to God.

The Catholic religion encompasses many diverse modes of worship—from the exotic rites of India, Africa, the Middle East and Eastern Europe to the charismatic movement to the contemplative movement. Personally I find great hope in the Byzantine Catholic doctrine of the "Deification of Man" and great freedom within the image-less form of contemplative prayer. If my religion appears to be different than yours, all that means is that our spiritual temperaments are different. Yet I take solace knowing that the course I have followed is also part of both of our religious roots.

FOR REFLECTION OR DISCUSSION

1. How important is it to you to be rooted?
2. What path have you followed on your spiritual journey?
3. Are you tolerant and appreciative of other people's paths?

Kathleen

teaches part-time, is married and the mother of three daughters. She likes popcorn, Walt Disney, and a shiny pair of shoes.

The Catholic Church claims historical continuity from Christ. I claim a continuity in my life within the Catholic Church.

As long as I can remember, the Catholic Church has been a part of my life. On Saturday nights my parents would have us put our shoes in the kitchen to be polished for church the next day. On Sunday morning we would rise early and attend church together, followed by a family meal and family activities—a visit to the Art Institute, airplane watching, fishing. The day almost always ended watching the Walt Disney show on T.V.

But my life wasn't a fairy tale, and in my 30's it became important to me what God was called. In the Bible I found references to God as female—in the story of the woman looking for the lost coins and as a female eagle, for example. I struggled with belonging to a Church that allows only male priests and uses exclusive language by referring to God as "He" and "King." I felt the Church was saying I wasn't as "Godlike" as men are. I visited other churches and read about other religions. In each I found human limitations. I'm stubborn and I decided that by definition alone (since "catholic" does mean broad in sympathies, tastes and interests) I could be part of the struggle to create that true community of Christ within the Catholic Church.

The Catholic Church to me is a bit like those scuffed shoes on Saturday nights. Well-worn, scratched, chipped, and roughened—but with real potential to shine. It is the possibilities that keep me Catholic.

FOR REFLECTION OR DISCUSSION

1. What practices, beliefs, or traditions from your childhood did you question or challenge as you matured?
2. How did this change you?
3. What is your image or idea of the "perfect" church or religion?

Kay

is an assistant registrar at a midwestern university, grew up on a farm, and is the fifth eldest in a family of thirteen.

My Catholic faith seems as essential a part of me as my heart. Somewhere, somehow, being raised Catholic made me want to remain Catholic, even during those college days when I rebelled against most other establishments. Of course, I had to make the transition from being a child Catholic at home to being an adult Catholic on my own.

When I happened to fall in love with a Lutheran, this development of my own faith provided the basis for my going beyond "you have to get married in the Church" to forming a true ecumenical marriage—a marriage our family and friends could accept and one that still endures. It's this same adult Catholicism that helps me accept my friends' beliefs without relinquishing mine.

Being Catholic has also helped me deal with the deaths of family and close friends. When my father died, I remember being glad he was Catholic. I saw a little smile on his face at the wake. Somehow that made me feel that life after death was real and that he was enjoying it.

I think once I knew I was always going to remain Catholic I could let my faith do some growing up. Today, being Catholic helps me through my anger, my frustrations, my disappointments—it's also there when I'm in total awe of what goes on around me. I don't sit and ponder being Catholic. I do ponder some deep sense in me I can never quite explain that keeps me trying to be a little better, pray a little harder, be a little more kind than yesterday.

I am Catholic because of that deeper sense that gives my soul what the bottom of my heart gives my body. If I didn't have the bottom of my heart, my life would simply drain out. If I didn't have my Catholicism, then my whole spiritual being would just fade away.

FOR REFLECTION OR DISCUSSION

1. At what age do you remember experiencing a situation or facing a decision for the first time "on your own"?
2. What did you learn from that experience?
3. Has that same experience occurred in your spiritual life? Explain.

Max

is a professional historian and "amateur" Christian, but always learning.

I'm Catholic because it gives me a sense of who I am and where I am in a world that is increasingly without reference points from which you can take bearings and know where you're going. Certitude is not available to anyone today—our world is too chaotic. But we can hope for a sense of direction amid the confusion of our times.

I have a sense of belonging to a continuum of religious experience, of being a member of a community of faith that reaches out over time and space. When I'm traveling in England, I can worship at the Brompton Oratory in London where John Henry Newman lived and prayed. Cardinal Newman lived a century before me, but I have a sense of continuing on this pilgrimage of faith toward one common destination.

My journey through history is never without the markers our spiritual ancestors left to guide our way. They were generous toward their successors, and they seemed to know we would need their help along a road filled with obstacles and distractions. A visit to Assisi can only remind one of St. Francis and his prayer that God make him an instrument of peace. Can anyone visit Sante Fe in our own Southwest without calling to mind Archbishop Lamy and his struggle to preserve our faith in desert places?

Whether the deserts be in the physical or spiritual realm, one of our Catholic predecessors has been there, marking the way, struggling with the same doubts, temptations, and difficulties I experience—giving me confidence that perseverance in faith is the way to salvation.

FOR REFLECTION OR DISCUSSION

1. From what ethnic background or backgrounds do you come?
2. Identify some of the "markers" left by your ancestors.
3. How would you say these ancestors have influenced your spiritual life today?

Pat

is a retired nurse educator now serving as a volunteer coordinator for the Mental Health Association.

I am Catholic because the Church gives me what I need when I need it. Now that I am older, I find myself among the "elders" of the parish—hard for me to believe, but it's true. I am certainly older than our priests, and that has always been a criterion of old age for me!

When I was a child and adolescent, the rules of Friday abstinence, Lenten fasting, and frequent confession were all still in place. I learned discipline and the rewards of self-control, and that lesson has served me well. During my college and work years, I was helped to develop spiritually through daily Mass, weekly devotions, novenas, silent retreats, and Benediction. These exercises offered me spiritual sustenance and positive suggestions for growth. I look back on them as being very helpful as well as a source of spiritual strength.

After my marriage and when my children were small, Pope John XXIII and Vatican II opened the Church windows and let the fresh breeze into our lives. There were fewer rules but more emphasis on "love thy neighbor." This helped me, just at the right time, to be more positive with my husband and children and gave us all a broader view—outward looking, more ecumenical, greater concern for others, and a religion not limited to self.

Our church started premarriage counseling, and my husband and I became involved. It brings such pleasure to see "our couples" coming to church now with their own children. We have taught confirmation classes and baked communion bread, knowing that the work of human hands allows the consecration to take place.

Now our own children are grown and a grandchild is on the way. I look forward eagerly to see what changes will take place in the Church that will cast reflections on our retirement years and on the lives of our children and grandchildren. How will the Church respond to me when I am old and frail? I am not anxious to find out, but so far the Church and I have grown together. I want to remain Catholic as we prayerfully progress.

My religion is not the same as when I was a child. The Church has helped me put away childish things, mature in my belief and practice, and begin new activities to enhance my faith. I think the Church can help me grow old with grace.

FOR REFLECTION OR DISCUSSION

1. How do you react to change in your life and in the world?

2. Give an example of someone or something that has been there for you with just what you needed.

3. How do you plan to grow old "gracefully"?

Jane

has lived through a lot, all of it while she was Catholic.

I was born into a strong God-fearing Catholic family in the "Baltimore Catechism" era, when to even think of being anything else would most certainly have doomed me to hell—or so I feared!

My years of Catholic education became my center of community within the Church. It was a kind of comfort zone where all my best friends were Catholic, and my teachers were my mentors and confidants. It was also an era of outward signs: the church processions, Stations of the Cross, the Rosary, May altars, First Communion, Benediction. All of this formed a reverence for God and love of the Church in my early years.

Then came the challenges or tests of my faith. Several children, an invalid grandmother to care for, the death of my husband, loneliness, fear, many days of bitterness and despair as to "why" all this happened to me. The charitable, communal dimensions of the Church reached out to me, clergy and laity all pulled together in many, many ways to get me over the "hump."

Gradually an inner peace or trust evolved in me that if this God in my community was indeed all merciful, as I had been taught, then if I trusted and prayed all would be well again. Then came another outward sign: a new love. My new love brought more children to me who were loved and gave so much love in return!

As I've grown in wisdom and years, my faith has been strengthened within my communal circle. This is certainly a gift. Not everyone is so lucky. I do believe it is God's gift to me for my acceptance of what has happened in my life. Sometimes my life has moved ahead, sometimes sideways, but always someone in the Church has moved with me. That is why I am still Catholic. The Church is my comfort zone, my best friend.

FOR REFLECTION OR DISCUSSION

1. Have you ever blamed God for your misfortune? How did you resolve your feelings?
2. Who reached out to help you in your need, and why?
3. Identify the comfort zones in your life. How is God present to you in them?

Jean Ann

is a business woman and new mother. She wrote this while watching her son begin to explore the world.

It would be easy to say I am Catholic because that's how I grew up, but that answer could only be half correct, since all five of my siblings had the same background yet—for reasons of their own—have left the Church.

I believe I am Catholic because the Catholic Church that I've experienced has been so diverse—allowing me to celebrate my faith in a variety of ways, yet all along keeping that stable unchanging framework the Church was built upon.

It's diverse. It's stable. A strange contradiction? No. Let me explain.

I grew up in a traditional worship setting that fostered discipline and stability in my faith. I learned about our Church and its history and how we all fit together. It was during the times that my faith was evolving that my Church, at the core, was stable and unchanging. It was like the parent who, acting in love, sets boundaries to follow.

As I grew physically and spiritually right within the same parish, however, I was able to explore another facet of my faith as a "hand-clappin'" charismatic at weekly prayer meetings, where I experienced God's spirit in new ways. Then, further down my life road I felt a need to live out my Christian faith more powerfully and so—still within the Catholic Church—I became involved in the Cursillo movement, where I joined with others to study and share Christ in my everyday life. I found a parish that celebrated liturgy in a very personal and uplifting way, which was what I needed as a young, single adult.

The doctrine of the Church is there to teach us about God and our relationship with God. To me, being part of the Catholic family means accepting this and then going forth in my life to seek God personally, knowing at some junctures I may have to look a bit harder to see where my Church and I fit together the best.

FOR REFLECTION OR DISCUSSION

1. What has provided stability in your life?
2. How has your faith evolved over the years?
3. In what ways do you still see your faith evolving today?

Tom

is an art history professor married to Barb, who continually sustains his belief in goodness in a blighted world.

My father was an Irish Catholic, my mother became a convert to Catholicism, and I attended Catholic grade and high school. Never an altar or choir boy, I nevertheless had no alternative to Catholicism.

Now that seems so very long ago, and I teasingly but truthfully tell my wife that the only life I remember begins with our life together and the rearing of our three children. The growth of my Catholic faith is inseparable from our shared beliefs. From the beginning we both brought to our marriage an unwavering commitment to the Church, which had nurtured us throughout our childhood and our youth. The Church provided us with a system of values that sustains and enhances our lives together.

Maturity has brought a deepening spiritual dimension to my life. I have become aware of deeper yearnings, more profound needs, a powerful "innerness" which must be acknowledged and nurtured. I don't devote time to spiritual reading, but I do try to pray daily, and I find the communal worship of my parish affirming. Being planted in the Catholic Church has been right for me from the beginning.

The Church also taught me to believe in miracles when I needed one. A crisis occurred in the form of a life-threatening illness to a family member. Thanks to God, the situation has improved dramatically. Had it been otherwise, I don't know what effect or disastrous conclusion it could have brought to my faith. But because our unceasing litany of prayer was answered by an astonishing return to health, I have chosen to regard this as a dramatic sign of God's love, goodness, and mercy—an irrefutable manifestation of God's presence in our lives. This return to health can be explained very simply, very matter-of-factly in terms of the results of competent medical treatment, but I prefer to interpret this as evidence of divine intervention, a miracle.

FOR REFLECTION OR DISCUSSION

1. Have you become aware of "deeper yearnings, more profound needs, a powerful 'innerness' which must be acknowledged and nurtured" as you grow older?
2. How is your spiritual life intertwined with that of another or others?
3. What do you believe about miracles? Have you ever experienced a miracle in your life?

Ann

is a homemaker and community volunteer.

The thing I love most about being Catholic is the liturgy. The beauty and holiness of the Catholic liturgy fill me with a sense of peace. Celebrating communion every week is important to me. It centers me and gives me the strength I need to accept the grace of God and live up to my values in my daily life.

The Catholic Church supports a strong value system centered on justice. Its history supplies us with many role models, people with the strength and courage to stand up for what they believe in. I want to share this with my children. The Church offers us the gift of heroes and heroines not found in popular culture.

A challenge I am given regularly by someone in my peer group is, "Give me one good reason why you're still Catholic!" I guess it all comes down to expectations. If you see the Church as made up only of "others"—of holy priests and saints—then it is easy to leave when it isn't perfect. But I believe the Church consists of real people with real problems, just like a family. And, as in my family, the reality of some things connected to the Church can sadden and disappoint me. But I don't give up on my family when it is imperfect and neither would I desert the Church.

FOR REFLECTION OR DISCUSSION

1. What are the regular, consistent events in your life that give you strength and peace?
2. When you are disillusioned by someone or something you believed in, how do you react?
3. Think about your expectations of religion in general and the Catholic Church in particular. Are they realistic or idealized? Why?

Ron

takes a long walk every day, during which, he says, "I often have long conversations with God, who listens more than speaks and always brings me home again."

I'm a Catholic because God wants me to be one. Even during some stretches of time when I did not want to be Catholic, God made me search out reasons why it would be a good idea if I stayed one. This is how God did it.

I grew up Catholic in a household in which being Catholic simply was part of being. It was a legacy, the same as my name, genetic code, and language.

When I had my first "I don't want to be" crisis in college, God introduced me to the works of C.S. Lewis. He taught me that secular education and knowledge and being Catholic were compatible. This intellectual dimension of my faith was reinforced by a large number of other writers ranging from Plato through Dostoevsky to Calvin and Hobbes (the comic strip). I got the message through all of these writers that being religious is the most essential need of human beings. Once that understanding was clear, God had me—again.

If books and scholarship didn't get the job done, people I encountered did. Both ordinary and extraordinary men and women who were searching for God modeled for me the fact that my being alive had a purpose that was a lot bigger than I wanted to acknowledge. I finally accepted the simple proposition that God had a purpose and place for me, and it would be a lot better for me simply to accept and live that fact.

When someone or something in the Church makes me cringe, God always sticks the word catholic—universality—in my head. All kinds of people belong to the Church. If the word universality doesn't work, sinful does. Where else would I be accepted when I sinned—which is quite often?

There are many other reasons I remain Catholic. There is the need to be connected to other people by something more than contracts. There is the need for beauty and inspiration. There is the need for a different vision of purpose in a screwed-up world. There is the need to be part of a human chain that goes back two thousand years, rooting me in something more than the ephemeral or the latest fad. And there is the need to keep caring in an uncaring world. God used every one of these reasons when I needed to be reminded what is really important in life.

I know I always had a choice. But deep down, I don't really feel I did. God wanted me to be a Catholic—and that was that.

FOR REFLECTION OR DISCUSSION

1. What is the role of ideas, intellect, and rational thought in your life?
2. What spiritual reading have you done? From what authors or books have you received inspiration, encouragement, insight, courage?
3. What do you think is the meaning of life?

Pat's

husband first noticed her on Christmas Eve when he was up in the choir loft and she was sitting with her mother in the front row of Saint Bernard's Church. He was 19, she was 18.

My mother's faith was so important to her she baptized me twice—once in the hospital shortly after I was born and again with the parish priest a week later.

It was my mother's Catholic faith that gave her life focus, meaning, and purpose. It answered her difficult questions and resolved her difficult problems. It gave her security. Her faith was so strong nothing shook it, not even the early death of her husband, leaving her a widow with four small children and no means of financial support. Each night she prayed the Rosary, asking for guidance, courage, and the strength she would need the next day. Each morning, when her children were old enough to be left on their own, she walked a mile to attend Mass. Years later, when my children wanted something special I would tell them to ask Grandma to pray for it. But, I would add, "You had better really want it, because God will not say no to Grandma."

As a teenager, my faith and my mother's example told me to wait for sex until after marriage; that the abuse of alcohol, drugs, or food is a sin; that stealing is wrong. I learned that faith and family are the most important things in my life and would see me through any crisis.

As an adult this faith saw me through four children in five years (a set of twins!) and helped me raise them. It gave me the strength to say no when a doctor suggested an abortion for a pregnancy that occurred at a bad time. Later, when I had a natural miscarriage, my faith gave me the strength to accept the death of my child because life and death are in God's hands.

I saw the importance of the Catholic faith in the living and dying of my mother, uncles, aunts, and grandparents. These lessons validated my faith, which gives structure and meaning to my life, as well as the strength to survive personal problems and make moral decisions. And this same faith will give me the courage to face my own death.

FOR REFLECTION OR DISCUSSION

1. Who is the person you know who has best modeled a strong and trusting faith? How did faith operate in that person's life?
2. What do you use to help you decide moral and ethical questions?
3. How do you deal with the certainty of death—that of your loved ones or even your own?

Richard

is a teacher who moved so often his daughter was thirteen before she understood they were Roman Catholics and not "Roamin' Catholics."

Among my earliest and most treasured Catholic memories are Holy Week, Saturday afternoon confessions, and hanging out with schoolmates at the parish recreation center. Year after year, until I left home, those times and places played an important part in shaping my religious character.

After many years of "peaks" and "valleys" on my Catholic journey through life, I still have vivid memories of those Good Fridays and Easter Sundays, those long lines leading to the confessional, and those penny loafers and pleated skirts at the Friday night dances. These images contain much of what has kept my Catholic faith alive.

Holy Week always brought out the humanness in us as we struggled to understand and accept our limitations, and even death itself. It seemed that many of our deepest feelings found expression during those days as we followed the final steps of Jesus, identifying with his own profound experience of the human condition. I think this annual return to the Last Supper, the Agony in the Garden, the trial and crucifixion, and the Resurrection of Jesus has helped me "keep the faith" more than anything else.

How can any of us old-timers forget those Saturday afternoon confessions? It all seems strange now, but for some reason that memory continues to have a hold on me. Although we don't do it as often anymore, confession still reminds me that to be forgiven and forgiving is an essential part of what it means to be Catholic.

Finally, we didn't call it "hanging out" in my day, but believe me we did a lot of it. Although I don't see many of those high-school classmates anymore, it was important to me then, as it is now, that we all felt a certain sense of community and could call upon one another in times of need.

I remain a Catholic for many more reasons than I can express here. I chose those three early memories because they connect so closely with the three distinctive teachings of our faith—the Incarnation, the Redemption, and the Trinity. God in Jesus assumed our finite human nature and raised it up. God through Jesus forgives us our sins. God—the Father, Son and Holy Spirit—is a community inviting us to share divine life.

I remain Catholic not because it's the only way, but because it's the way that was given to me. I am grateful for that.

FOR REFLECTION OR DISCUSSION

1. What is your strongest memory from childhood relating to God, Church or religion?
2. What gifts from your childhood remain precious to you even today?
3. What do human dignity, forgiveness, and community mean to you?

Chuck

is a husband, father, and teacher educator whose life regularly touches others in many different ways.

My first serious contact with Catholicism occurred when I began dating the girl who was to eventually become my wife. I began attending Mass frequently with Sue, and she answered many of my questions about this new experience. I slowly gained an admiration of her tremendous faith and understanding. She had been raised Catholic through family, church, and school. I wondered why I didn't have an equal understanding of my church even though I had always been a regular participant.

At the age of twenty-two, I decided to seriously pursue my growing interest in the Church. It was actually my insurance agent who introduced me to the priest who gave me a catechism, which led me to becoming Catholic. I was amazed at how easily I could accept his instructions. Was I just gullible? Or had I really found something my soul was searching for all along? Whatever, I decided to join the Church. I have never been sorry.

Without doubt, the reason I remain Catholic is because of the internal support I have been given during my struggles with life. When it might have been easier to look at the glass as half empty, my faith has provided me with a sense of optimism and the conviction that the glass is half full. When I have felt frustrated and angry, my faith has given me a sense of compassion and understanding. When I think I have been treated unfairly by someone, this feeling is quickly erased as I picture Jesus being marched to his own death.

There is great consolation in knowing that, wherever I travel, I can always find a place to attend Mass and receive the body and blood of our Lord. And, how empty Christmas and Easter would be without the knowledge of Jesus' presence!

While the Catholic faith has helped me make my own life more comfortable, it has also given me direction in fulfilling my obligations toward others. The simple understanding that God is all around us has helped me develop a sense of responsibility toward my family in particular and society in general.

Without faith there is no real Church. With it, there is reason to be Catholic.

FOR REFLECTION OR DISCUSSION

1. What does "faith" mean to you? Name some things you believe in.
2. How much do you know about the religion in which you were raised? How do you attempt to learn more about your faith?
3. What are your obligations toward others? Where do they come from?

Donna

works in a media development center, preserves her own jams and jellies, and has bravely begun piano lessons.

There is a difference between Catholic with a big "C" and catholic with a small "c." Catholic with a small "c" means universal, involving all, of interest to all. To me, catholic with a small "c" represents those unchanging, universal truths and principles that we live by: love your neighbor; turn the other cheek; seek to listen, console, and understand. Nowhere are these truths more evident to me than in my weekly visits to my surrogate grandmother. Although not Catholic with a big "C," she embodies what living "catholic" is all about.

Although she lives in poverty, she doesn't know it. The winter wind sneaking in the windows is "communing with the great outdoors." When a summer storm is coming, so does her "friend" Arthur(itis), who cripples her hands so badly she can't play her beloved piano. Headphones attached to an amplifier serve as her hearing aid. Not long ago she expressed her concern for her twenty-seven-year-old car "Matilda," who at her advanced age has taken up smoking! She added, however, that Matilda has grown friendlier with age. She now waves her rust-loosened fenders at all the cute, young sports cars.

Grandma puts her stock in the small goodness of each day. She's the first to decorate for each season and the last to take the paper trimmings down. She always has a holiday-of-the-month treat for the children: peanuts, apples, or a package of their favorite snack cakes that she divides among them. Like the biblical widow who contributed the mite, my grandmotherly friend is always giving us something: a pretty jelly jar, a trinket from her past, or a tune from the piano. She would not hesitate to give away her second winter coat—if she had one. Her positive attitude and honest goodness inspire me to keep my priorities in order amidst all the hustle and bustle. Her example encourages me to live catholic, with a small "c."

Of course, she's not the only influence on me. As a Catholic with a big "C," the traditions of the Church and the model of my brother Jesus play a large role in my Catholicity. I find rich faith experiences whether I am in my own parish or the Seattle Cathedral or the Vincent de Paul Center in Dallas or the small brick church planted amongst the cornfields in rural Wisconsin. All of these experiences influence my life choices. Being Catholic with a big "C" keeps me catholic with a small "c."

FOR REFLECTION OR DISCUSSION

1. What have you learned from people who believe differently than you?
2. How "catholic" with a small "c" are you?
3. What do you think Jesus meant when he said, "Blessed are the poor"?